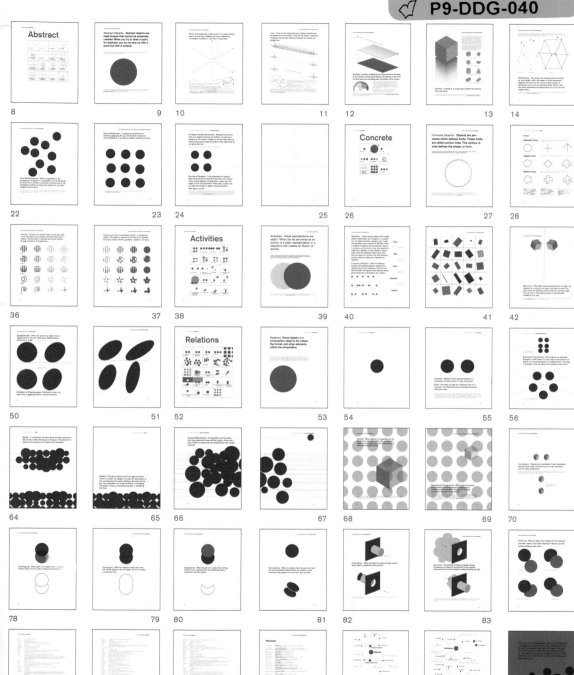

Princeton Architectural Press
37 East Seventh Street
New York, New York 10003

For a free catalog of books, call 1.800.722.6657.

Visit our Web site at www.papress.com.

First published in Norway by Abstrakt Forlag
in 2004

10 09 08 07 06 5 4 3 2 1 First edition

For Princeton Architectural Press:

Project editing: Nicola Bednarek
Design: Christian Leborg
Translation: Diane Oatley

Special thanks to: Nettie Aljian, Dorothy Ball, Janet Behning, Becca
Casbon, Penny (Yuen Pik) Chu, Russell Fernandez, Jan Haux, Clare
Jacobson, John King, Mark Lamster, Nancy Eklund Later, Linda Lee,
Katharine Myers, Lauren Nelson, Scott Tennent, Jennifer Thompson,
Paul Wagner, Joseph Weston, and Deb Wood of Princeton Architectural
Press —Kevin C. Lippert, publisher

Library of Congress Cataloging-in-Publication Data
Leborg, Christian.
  [Visuell grammatikk. English]
  Visual grammar / Christian Leborg.
      p. cm.
  Includes bibliographical references.
  ISBN-13: 978-1-56898-581-7 (alk. paper)
  ISBN-10: 1-56898-581-9 (alk. paper)
  1. Visual perception. 2. Visual communication in art. I. Title.
  N7430.5.L3913 2006
  701'.8—dc22
                                                    2005034807

Christian Leborg
Visual Grammar

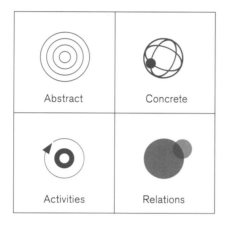

Abstract

Concrete

Activities

Relations

Princeton Architectural Press
New York

To Marianne

Preface

Every day we are confronted with vast amounts of visual messages, but without a basic understanding of visual language many of these messages remain incomprehensible to us, and a productive dialogue between producers and consumers of visual communication cannot take place.

Knowledge of visual concepts is often acquired through physical experience and applied without the use of written or spoken language; there are, however, a number of underlying processes before and after the act of creation where verbal language has an important function. Reflection about what one is going to create or what one has created alters the creative process: we think differently when we have a language to describe something. This book is a contribution towards establishing such a language. It intends to be both a primer on visual language and a visual dictionary of the fundamental aspects of visual communication.

The reason for writing a grammar of visual language is the same as for any language: to define its basic elements, describe its patterns and processes, and to understand the relations between the individual elements in the system. Visual language has no formal syntax or semantics, but the visual objects themselves can be classified. Accordingly, the book is divided into four parts: abstract objects and structures, concrete objects and structures, activities, and relations. The first chapter deals with abstractions such as dimension, format, and volume; the second concerns concrete objects and structures such as form, size, color, and texture; the third part describes the activities that can take place in a composition such as repetition, mirroring, and movement, and the fourth chapter deals with the relations between several objects in a composition.

Writing this book I have stood on the shoulders of a number of the greats who have thought and written about visual language. They are listed in the selected bibliography at the back of the book. I would also like to thank Anette Wang, who gave me resistance when I needed it and my Norwegian publisher Einar Plyhn, who gave me no resistance whatsoever. Yngve Lien and Bjørn Kruse contributed constructive criticism. In addition, I received valuable feedback from professionals and laymen, friends and family.

I hope that this book will help you speak and write about visual objects and their creative potential and enable you to better understand the graphics that you encounter every day.

Oslo, November 2005
Christian Leborg

Abstract

Abstract Objects

10   Point

11   Line

12   Surface

13   Volume

14   Dimensions

16   Format

Abstract Structures

19   Formal Structures

20   Gradation

21   Radiation

22   Informal Structures

23   Visual Distribution

24   Invisible/Inactive Structures

24   Structural Skeleton

Concrete

Concrete Objects

28   Form

30   Size

32   Color

Concrete Structures

35   Visible Structures

35   Active Structures

36   Texture

Activities

40   Repetition

40   Frequency/Rhythm

42   Mirroring

43   Mirroring against a Volume

44   Rotation

46   Upscaling/Downscaling

48   Movement

48   Path

49   Direction

49   Superordinate/Subordinate Movement

50   Displacement

50   Direction of Displacement

Relations

55   Attraction

55   Static

56   Symmetry/Asymmetry

57   Balance

58   Groups

60   Fine/Coarse

61   Diffusion

62   Direction

63   Position

64   Space

65   Weight

66   Amount/Dominance

68   Neutral

69   Background/Foreground

70   Coordination

71   Distance

72   Parallel

73   Angle

74   Negative/Positive

75   Transparent/Opaque

76   Tangent

78   Overlapping

79   Compound

80   Subtraction

81   Coincidence

82   Penetration

83   Extrusion

84   Influence

85   Modification

86   Variation

89   Glossary

96   Bibliography

Abstract

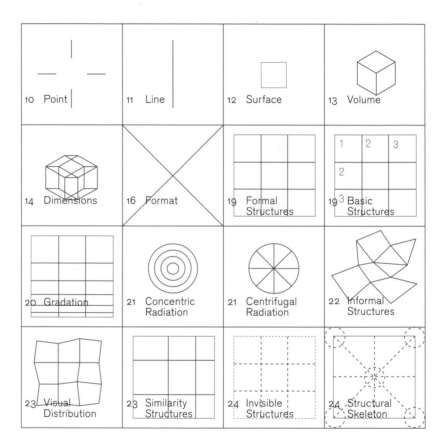

10 Point	11 Line	12 Surface	13 Volume
14 Dimensions	16 Format	19 Formal Structures	19³ Basic Structures
20 Gradation	21 Concentric Radiation	21 Centrifugal Radiation	22 Informal Structures
23 Visual Distribution	23 Similarity Structures	24 Invisible Structures	24 Structural Skeleton

Abstract Objects. Abstract objects are ideal shapes that cannot be physically created. When you try to draw a point, for example, you do not end up with a point but with a surface.

·

The above illustration may look like a point, but it is only the representation of a point. It is actually a dot with a surface. Its size is 0.1% of that of the illustration below.

"The abstract conveys the essential meaning, cutting through the conscious to the unconscious, from experience of the substance in the sensory field directly to the nervous system, from the event to perception." Donis A. Dondis, *A Primer of Visual Literacy.* (Cambridge: MIT Press, 1973), 81.

Point. ~~You cannot~~ see or feel a point; it is a place without area. The point has a position that can be defined by coordinates (numbers on one, two, or three axes).

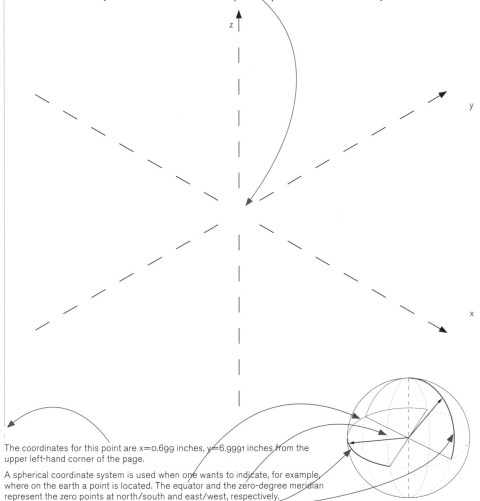

The coordinates for this point are x=0.699 inches, y=6.9991 inches from the upper left-hand corner of the page.

A spherical coordinate system is used when one wants to indicate, for example, where on the earth a point is located. The equator and the zero-degree meridian represent the zero points at north/south and east/west, respectively.

"The geometric point is an invisible thing. Therefore, it must be defined as an incorporeal thing. Considered in terms of substance, it equals zero." Wassily Kandinsky, *Point and Line to Plane* (New York: Dover, 1979), 25. First published in 1926 as *Punkt und Linie zu Fläche* in a series of Bauhaus books edited by Walter Gropius and L. Moholy-Nagy.

Line. A line can be understood as a number of points that are adjacent to one another. A line can be infinite or have two endpoints. The shortest distance between two points is a straight line.

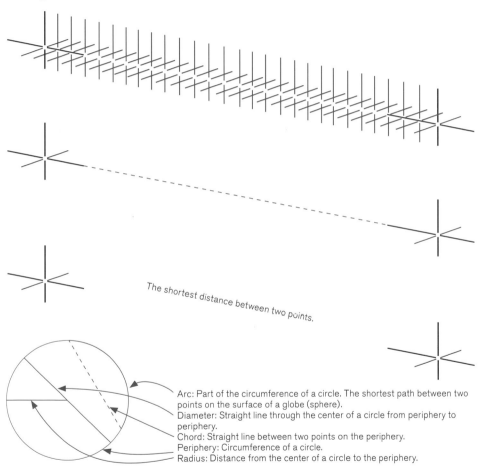

The shortest distance between two points.

Arc: Part of the circumference of a circle. The shortest path between two points on the surface of a globe (sphere).
Diameter: Straight line through the center of a circle from periphery to periphery.
Chord: Straight line between two points on the periphery.
Periphery: Circumference of a circle.
Radius: Distance from the center of a circle to the periphery.

"Line rarely exists in nature. But line does appear in the environment: the crack in the sidewalk, telephone wires against the sky, bare branches in winter, a cable bridge. The visual element of line is used mostly to express the juxtaposition of two tones. Line is utilized most often to describe that juxtaposition, and in this, it is an artificial device." Dondis, *A Primer of Visual Literacy*, 44.

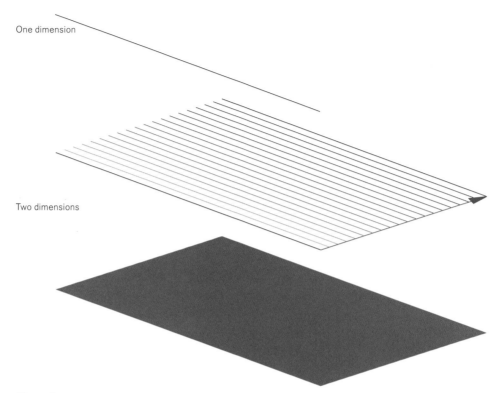

One dimension

Two dimensions

Surface. A surface is defined by two lines that do not coincide or by a minimum of three points that are not located on a line. If the two lines have one coinciding point, the surface will be a plane.

In the same way that a line can be described as a row of adjacent points, a surface can be defined as a row of lines. Points are stacked in one direction to form a line; a surface is created when a row of lines is stacked at a right angle to that direction. These directions can also be seen as axes and dimensions. Because a surface is a point that is proliferated in two directions, a surface has two dimensions.

The outside of a volume is a surface. It can be a continuous surface with different curves, or a collection of polygons, or a multiangular surface such as the figure on the left.

"The path of a line in motion becomes a plane. A plane has length and breadth, but no thickness. It has position and direction. It is bound by lines. It defines the external limits of a volume." Wucius Wong, *Principles of Form and Design* (New York: Van Nostrand Reinhold, 1993), 42.

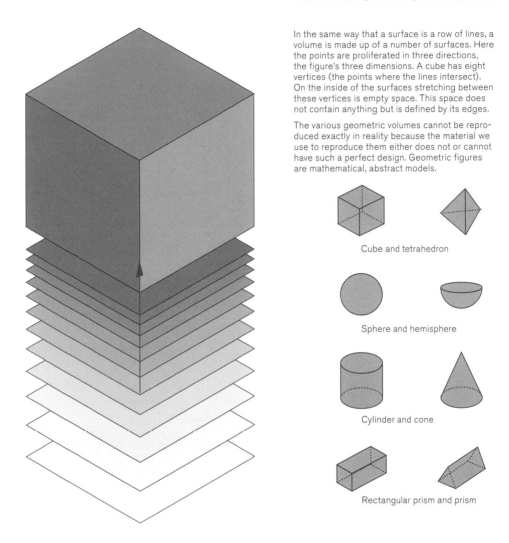

In the same way that a surface is a row of lines, a volume is made up of a number of surfaces. Here the points are proliferated in three directions, the figure's three dimensions. A cube has eight vertices (the points where the lines intersect). On the inside of the surfaces stretching between these vertices is empty space. This space does not contain anything but is defined by its edges.

The various geometric volumes cannot be reproduced exactly in reality because the material we use to reproduce them either does not or cannot have such a perfect design. Geometric figures are mathematical, abstract models.

Cube and tetrahedron

Sphere and hemisphere

Cylinder and cone

Rectangular prism and prism

Volume. A volume is an empty space defined by surfaces, lines, and points.

"The path of a plane in motion (in a direction other than its intrinsic directon), becomes a volume. It has a position in space and is bound by planes. In two-dimensional design, volume is illusory." Wong, *Principles of Form and Design,* 42.

A line has one edge, two vertices, and one dimension. A surface with four edges has four vertices and two dimensions. A cube has twelve edges, eight vertices, six surfaces, and three dimensions. A hypercube has thirty-two edges, sixteen vertices, twenty-four surfaces, and four dimensions.

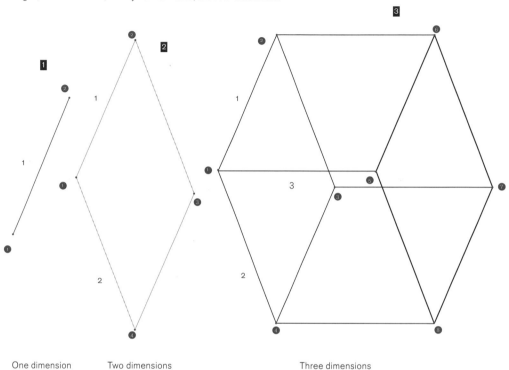

One dimension   Two dimensions   Three dimensions

Dimensions. We, along with everything that surrounds us, have height, width, and depth—or three dimensions. Objects can have four, five, and an infinite number of dimensions, but we cannot perceive these. More or less than three dimensions are abstractions for us; we can only imagine them.

"Dimension exists in the real world. We cannot only feel it, but with the aid of our two-eyed, stereoopticon sight, we can see it." Dondis, *A Primer of Visual Literacy*, 59–60.

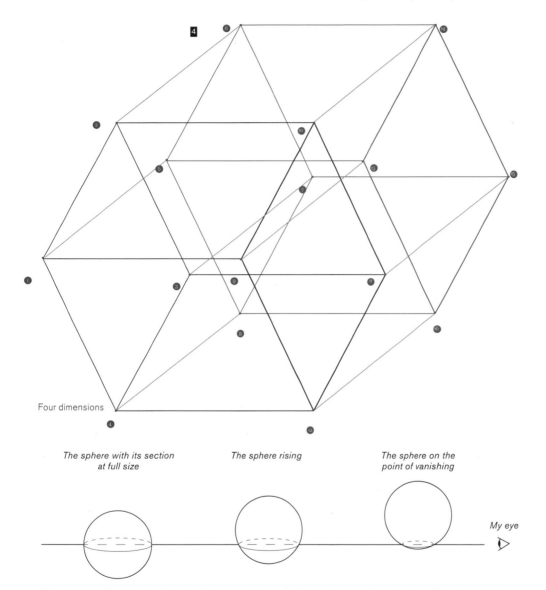

Four dimensions

The sphere with its section
at full size

The sphere rising

The sphere on the
point of vanishing

My eye

Edwin Abbott Abbott's book *Flatland* tells the story of a square that lives in a two-dimensional world together with its family of geometric figures. One day a three-dimensional sphere comes to visit. When the square tells the clergy about meeting someone from another dimension, it is imprisoned for blasphemy. Above we see the sphere's visit as viewed by the square. Illustration based on Abbott's drawing. Edwin Abbott Abbott, *Flatland* (London: Seeley & Co, 1884).

F

When designing a book, it can be expedient to select a format or trim size that is based on the proportions of the letters with which the book is to be typeset.

Format. Everything we see is experienced in relation to its external limits. If we could not relate visual signals to a format—in other words, to a surface, a space, or a limitation in time—our brain would not be able to interpret any of these impressions.

"Format (lat. *formet*) 1. size of a piece of paper or book, 2. scope, size." R. Broby-Johansen, *Kunst ordbog*. Newly revised and expanded edition (Viborg: Forlaget Sesam, 2000), 65.

The term *format* can be used to refer to dimensions, proportions, and scales of measurement.

Examples are typographic measurements, metric measurements (meter, centimeter, millimeter), Anglo-American measurements (feet and inches), map formats, architectonic formats, paper formats, book formats, newspaper formats, poster formats, film formats, screen formats, etc.

Screen formats are usually measured in pixels; a pixel (picture element) is the smallest unit of information in digital images. They are quadratic and about 0.0139 inches in size.

Typographic points (abbreviated as pt.) are the smallest typographic units, measuring approximately 0.0148 inches. The cicero is the central unit of measurement in the typographic system, comprising twelve typographic points.

The formats for maps and architectural plans are expressed as the ratio between the drawing and the physical size, for example 1 : 50 000 000, 1 : 50.

In Europe paper formats follow the DIN system, which is based on the root 2 rectangle, and are called A, B, and C.

Most book formats are based on the golden section or golden mean, a mathematic formula that expresses the ratio between two sizes, in this case between the height and width of a page. The golden section is achieved when one divides a line segment such that the ratio of the shorter line to the longer line is the same as the ratio of the longer line to the whole segment. See the formula below and the model on the right.

$$\frac{c}{b} = \frac{b}{a}$$

This ratio, $\frac{\sqrt{5}+1}{2}$ or 1.618, also appears in the so called Fibonacci sequence, where each number in the sequence is the sum of the two preceding numbers: 1, 2, 3, 5, 8, 13, 21, 34, 55, 89… The ratio of adjacent numbers in the sequence progressively approaches 1:1.618.

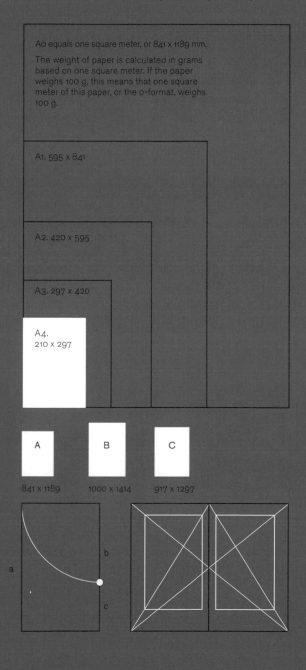

A0 equals one square meter, or 841 x 1189 mm.

The weight of paper is calculated in grams based on one square meter. If the paper weighs 100 g, this means that one square meter of this paper, or the 0-format, weighs 100 g.

A1. 595 x 841

A2. 420 x 595

A3. 297 x 420

A4.
210 x 297

A
841 x 1189

B
1000 x 1414

C
917 x 1297

Abstract Structures. Placing objects in relation to one another will establish a structure. We can only describe a structure if we are able to recognize its pattern. A structure that does not have visible structure lines is called abstract.

Formal Structures. When objects are evenly distributed in a composition, the structure is formal. The axes according to which the objects are organized are called structure lines.

Structure lines can pass through the objects' center or optical center. They can also run between the objects and define larger structural elements within which the objects are placed.

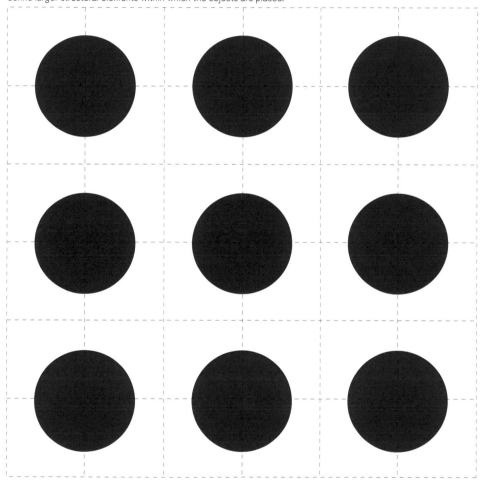

A structure in which all sections or objects are alike and equally distributed is called a basic structure or a grid. This kind of repetitive structure is based on structure lines that are perpendicular to one another, usually horizontally and vertically.

Gradation. A gradated structure works in the same way as a repetitive structure, but here the structure units change in size or form (or both) at an even rate.

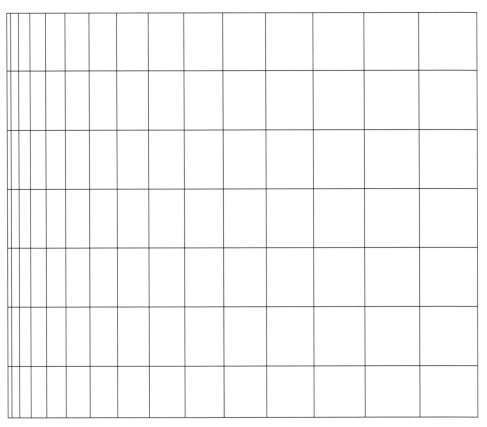

Parallel

Radiation

Gradation can apply to distance, change in angle, displacement, and curve.

On the left some of the most common gradated structures are shown: parallel gradation (lines running in the same direction) and radiation (expanding from a center).

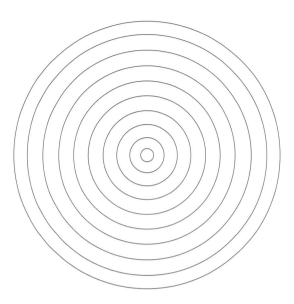

We speak of concentric radiation when the structure lines are circles with an unequal distance from the same center.

Radiation. A radiation is a formal repetitive structure with structure units that are situated around a common center.

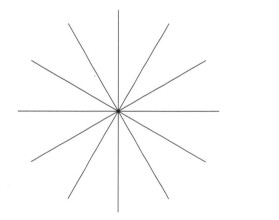

The spiral is concentric in that its structure lines have an unequal distance from the center. It is also centrifugal because the helical line emerges from a center. The spiral is thus a hybrid between a concentric and centrifugal structure.

We speak of centrifugal radiation when the structure lines diverge from a common center.

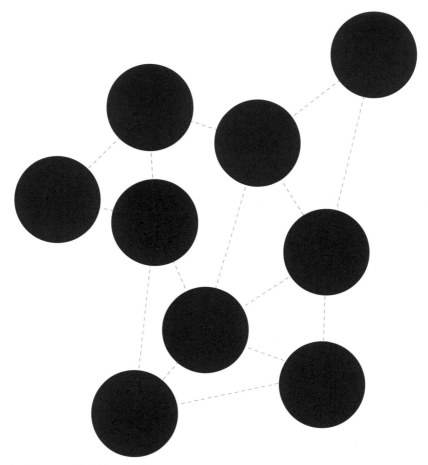

Informal Structures. When no regularities in the arrangement of objects in a composition can be discerned, the structure is informal. A structure is informal even if one recognizes a pattern as long as the objects do not follow straight structure lines.

It is likely that parts of the structure above are formal even though we cannot recognize the pattern. There are some mathematic equations that when represented visually do not appear to have a formal structure. The definitions here concern only the visual aspects of structures.

Visual Distribution. If objects are positioned in a structure judging by the eye, the structure is based on visual distribution. It can also be called a similarity structure.

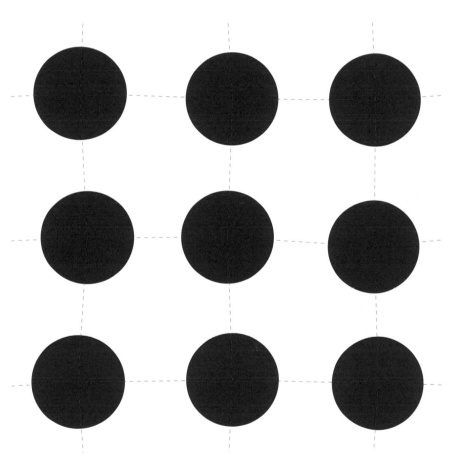

"Visual distribution should allow each unit form to occupy a similar amount of space as judged by the eye."
Wong, *Principles of Form and Design,* 42.

Invisible/Inactive Structures. Although the structure lines in an abstract structure are invisible, our brain has a tendency to fill in what is missing, so we see where they are. Inactive structures indicate the position of the objects but do not affect their form.

Inactive structures can be visible and invisible. (See also Active Structures, p. 35.)

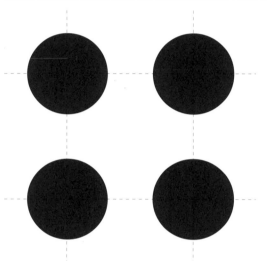

Structural Skeleton. In all compositions or objects there are forces that are bound by the limits of the surface. These varying degrees of energy follow certain axes with regard to form and proportions. These axes, or paths, can be called the format's or object's structural skeleton. (See figure on p. 25).

"So the nature of a visual experience cannot be described in terms of inches of size and distance, degrees of angle, or wave lengths of hue. These static measurements define only the 'stimulus,' that is, the message sent to the eye by the physical world. But the life of a percept—its expression and meaning—derives entirely from the activity of the perceptual forces." Rudolf Arnheim, *Art and Visual Perception* (Berkeley: University of California Press, 1964), 16.

Concrete

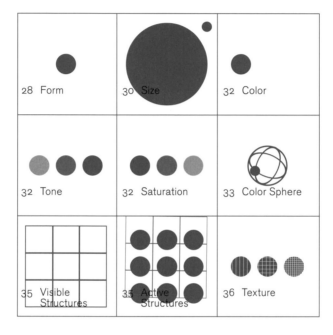

28 Form

30 Size

32 Color

32 Tone

32 Saturation

33 Color Sphere

35 Visible Structures

35 Active Structures

36 Texture

Concrete Objects. Objects are perceived within defined limits. These limits are called contour lines. The contour is what defines the shape, or form.

A surface can have many forms. Forms are defined by their contours, which can be straight or curved. If the visual transition is gradated or has small nuances in shade or hue, it is difficult to define the form.

"Form (from Lat. forma) 1. in common use, the exterior of a thing, 2. concrete: a round, square-shaped, etc. f., 3. Plastic, having volume, 4. Figuratively speaking, of an artwork's overall appearance as a visible object, without consideration for content, 5. Casting mould." Broby-Johansen, *Kunstordbog*, 65.

Form

Geometric forms

Geometric forms are based on mathematical facts about points, lines, surfaces, and solids.

Organic forms

Organic forms are created by living organisms or based on living organisms.

Random forms

Random forms are created through reproduction, unconscious human action, or incidental influence from nature.

Circle.
Astrology: Eternal, life. *Astronomy:* Full moon. *Meteorology:* Clear weather. *Cartography:* City, juncture. *Electricity:* Meter. *Chemistry:* Acid. *Mechanics:* Point of rotation. *Biology:* She.

Equal-armed Cross.
Astrology: Matter, the earthly. *Astronomy:* North. *Alchemy:* The four elements. *Cartography:* Church, chapel. *Dualistic terminology system:* Positive pole, plus sign, positive charge, increase.

Arrow.
Direction, logical consequence. Masculine gender. *Meteorology:* Frost in fog. *Physics:* Gravitational center. *Cartography:* Oceanic currents. *Runes:* Bull.

The forms presented here are some of the basic gestalts in Western ideography according to Carl G. Liungman (see his book *Symboler,* Malmö: Aldebaran Förlag, 1990). They are the basic signs man has created as complete legible entities.

  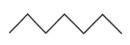

  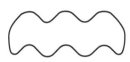

Square.
Materialization, the Earth.
Meteorology: The ground.
Cartography: Farm. *Biology:* He.
Military: Soldier. *Alchemy:* Salt.
Household article: Stop.

Heart.
Icon for the physical heart. Love,
to love. Ideogram for lavatory.

Water.

Size. The size of an object is relative to the person perceiving it and his or her perspective. The size of an object must be evaluated in relation to its placement and the format in which it will function.

This rectangle is 0.1‰ of a spread in this book.

Color. Colors are different wavelengths of light. Concrete objects and the materials of which they are made reflect only part of the light spectrum and therefore appear as if they have color.

Hue refers to the wavelength of the color and is separate from its intensity or saturation. Saturated hues are those we are accustomed to seeing in the chromatic circle. This book is printed in two colors, but only one hue, namely, red. Black, gray, and white are colors without hue.

Tone describes a color's lightness/darkness. The tone, also called the shade, is the color's content of black.

Saturation describes the relative ratio of the color's hue and white content. A color with little saturation contains a large amount of white.

"The seven kinds of color contrasts are the following: 1. Contrast of hue 2. Light-dark contrast 3. Cold-warm contrast 4. Complementary contrast 5. Simultaneous contrast 6. Contrast of saturation 7. Contrast of extension." Johannes Itten, *The Art of Color* (New York: Reinhold Publishing Corporation, 1967).

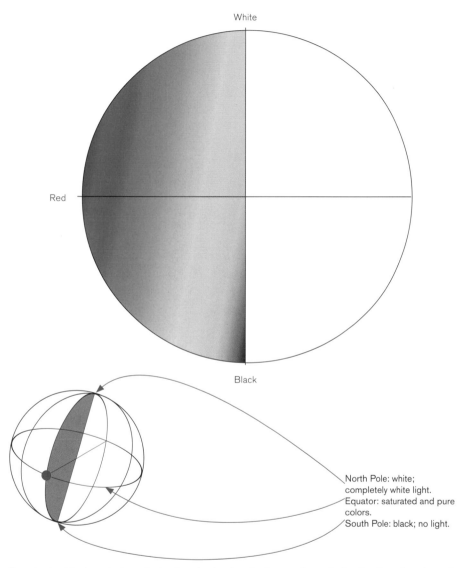

White

Red

Black

North Pole: white;
completely white light.
Equator: saturated and pure
colors.
South Pole: black; no light.

To understand the hue, shade, and saturation of colors, imagine them as the content and surface of a sphere where the North Pole is completely white and the South Pole completely black. The completely saturated and pure hues are located along the equator. If one moves in towards the center of the sphere, the colors will become less saturated and gradually be replaced by gray shades. On the surface of the southern hemisphere there are completely saturated colors with varying black content. (See also Itten, *The Art of Color.*)

Concrete Structures. A structure is concrete when its structure lines are visible or actively influence the form of the objects in the structure. In contrast to abstract structures, which only indirectly indicate how objects are positioned, concrete structures are visual compositions in themselves.

Visible Structures. A visible structure is a structure with visible structure lines. A visible structure can consist of structure lines and objects or of structure lines only.

Active Structures. A structure is active when the structure lines influence the form of the objects in the structure. A structure need not be visible to be active.

Texture.

A texture is a structure than can be seen and/or felt. The texture can consist of structure lines and/or objects. Texture exists in materials and can be created through inscription and application.

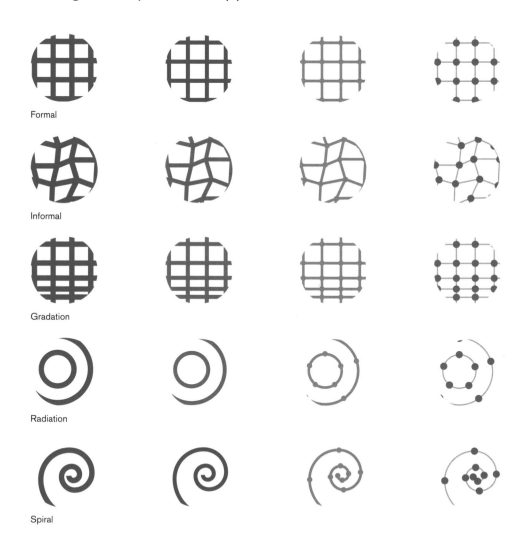

Formal

Informal

Gradation

Radiation

Spiral

Textures can have an ornamental, random, or mechanical design. The system of textures is the same as for abstract structures: formal, informal, gradation, radiation, and spiral.

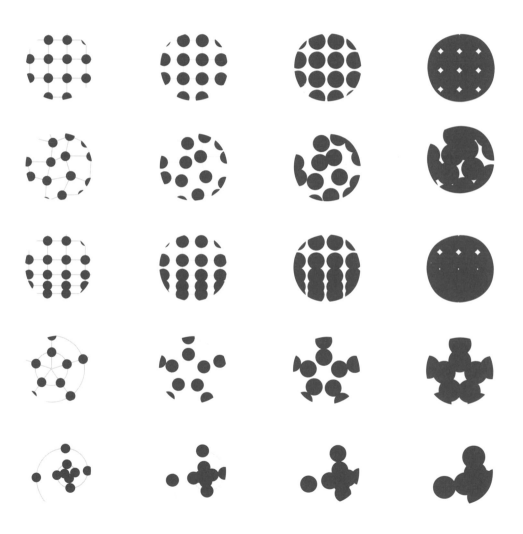

Activities

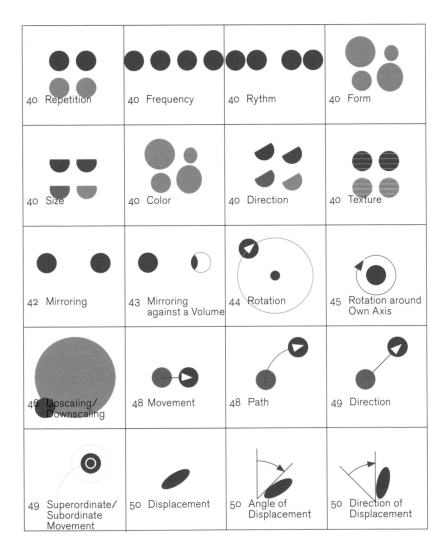

40 Repetition	40 Frequency	40 Rythm	40 Form
40 Size	40 Color	40 Direction	40 Texture
42 Mirroring	43 Mirroring against a Volume	44 Rotation	45 Rotation around Own Axis
46 Upscaling/ Downscaling	48 Movement	48 Path	49 Direction
49 Superordinate/ Subordinate Movement	50 Displacement	50 Angle of Displacement	50 Direction of Displacement

Activities. Visual reproductions are static*. What can be perceived as an activity, is a static representation or a sequence that creates an illusion of activity.

*Kinetic art—art that uses analog movement as an instrument—is the only genre within pictorial and visual art where the illusion of movement is not created with sequences of pictures or static representations. Film consists of still images shown in a series at a high frequency.

"Somewhere between the futurists' dynamic movement and Duchamp's diagrammatic concept of movement lies comics' 'Motion line.'" Scott McCloud, *Understanding Comics* (New York: Paradox Press, 1993), 110.

Repetition. When several objects with a single shared characteristic are arranged in a composition, the object has been repeated, even if other characteristics of the objects are different. When a multitude of objects has one particular feature in common, such as form or size, this repetition is called form repetition or size repetition, respectively. When the repeated objects have more than one feature in common, the most dominant common feature is selected to describe the repetition.

Frequency/Rhythm. When the distance between the repeated objects is identical, the repetition has an even frequency. When the distance between the objects varies between several given frequencies, the repetition has a rhythm.

Form

Size

Color

Even frequency

Direction

Uneven frequency

Texture

Rhythm

40

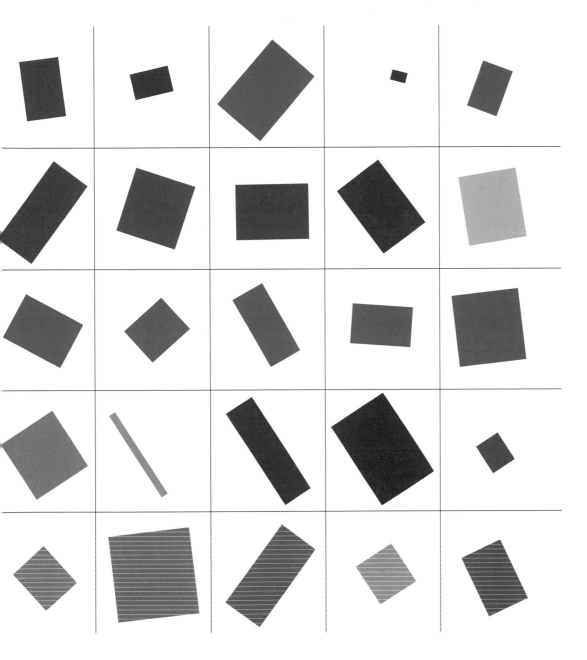

Mirroring.
When light waves emanating from an object are reflected on a surface, the object has been mirrored. The light waves are reflected off the surface at the same angle they fall onto it. The physical object is symmetrically rendered on an axis.

"A mirror doesn't reflect things the wrong way round, it reflects what is immediately in front of it." Alan Fletcher, *The Art of Looking Sideways* (London: Phaidon Press, 2001), 229.

Mirroring against a Volume. When the surface on which something is reflected has several different angles, it can be defined as a volume or as part of a volume. A volume that mirrors another object distorts the mirror image because the light that meets the surface is reflected at different angles.

Rotation. When an object moves around a point or an axis, it rotates. The shape of the path along which a rotating object moves can be either circular or elliptic.

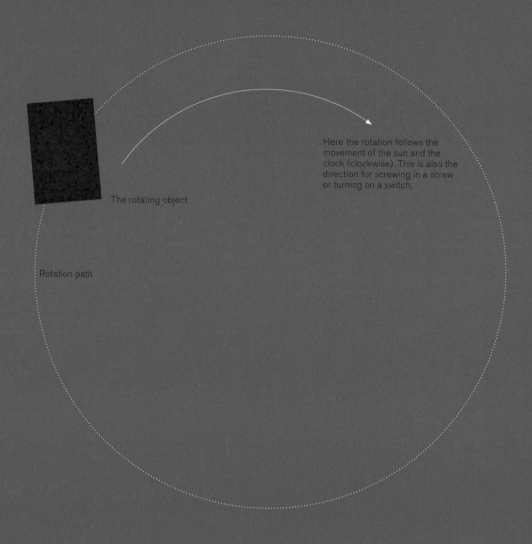

The rotating object

Here the rotation follows the movement of the sun and the clock (clockwise). This is also the direction for screwing in a screw or turning on a switch.

Rotation path

If the rotating object faces the rotation
point with the same side at all times,
the object will have rotated around itself
after one revolution.

The distance from the center to the
object's rotation path is called the pendulum. This distance is the radius of a circle.

The rotation point is the
center of a circle. In case
of an elliptical movement
the length of the pendulum
will vary.

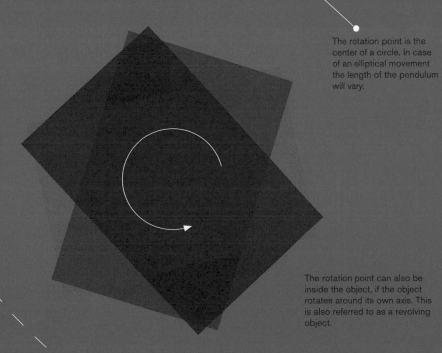

The rotation point can also be
inside the object, if the object
rotates around its own axis. This
is also referred to as a revolving
object.

Upscaling/Downscaling.

Objects are enlarged or scaled down along the x-axis and the y-axis. These directions are called horizontal and vertical, or level and perpendicular. When an object is enlarged or scaled down proportionately, the width-to-height ratio will remain constant.

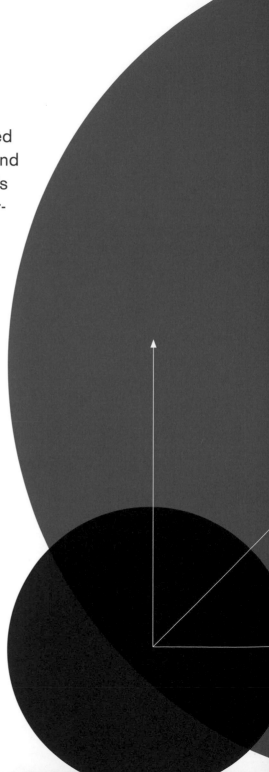

Movement.
True movement (without sequences or steps) is only found in the real world. Movement within a visual composition is only a representation of movement. The positioning of an object can suggest forces that have influenced or will influence it and move it.

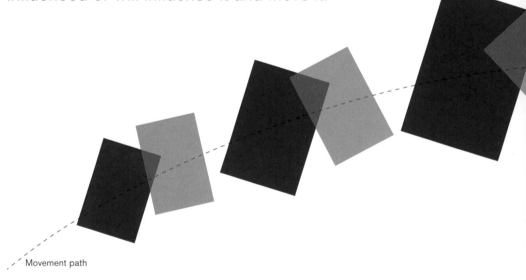

Movement path

Path.
An object in constant movement will travel along an imagined line. This line is called a path. The path can be straight or have the form of an arc.

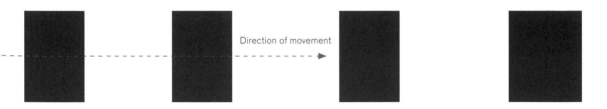

Direction of movement

Direction. The direction of a movement can be defined by the line that leads from the starting point of the movement to its presumed endpoint.

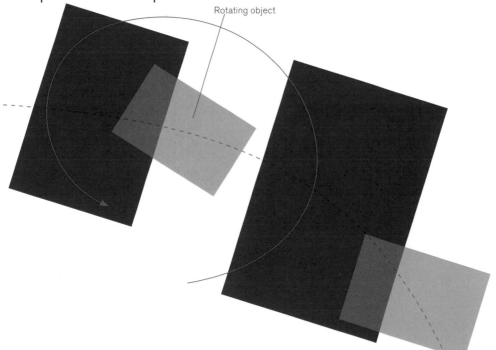

Rotating object

Superordinate and Subordinate Movement. An object can rotate, swing, or move forward and backward, while still experiencing a superordinate movement along one path.

Displacement. When only parts of an object move, a displacement of the form takes place. Displacement is defined by an angle.

Angle of displacement

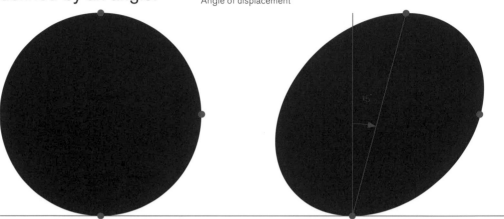

Direction and angle of displacement

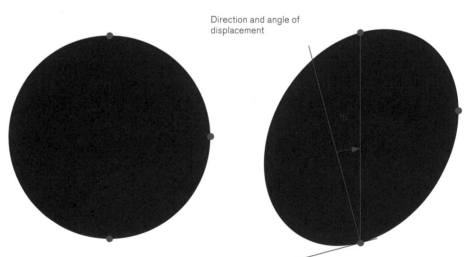

Direction of Displacement. The points or lines of an object that is displaced move in a specific direction.

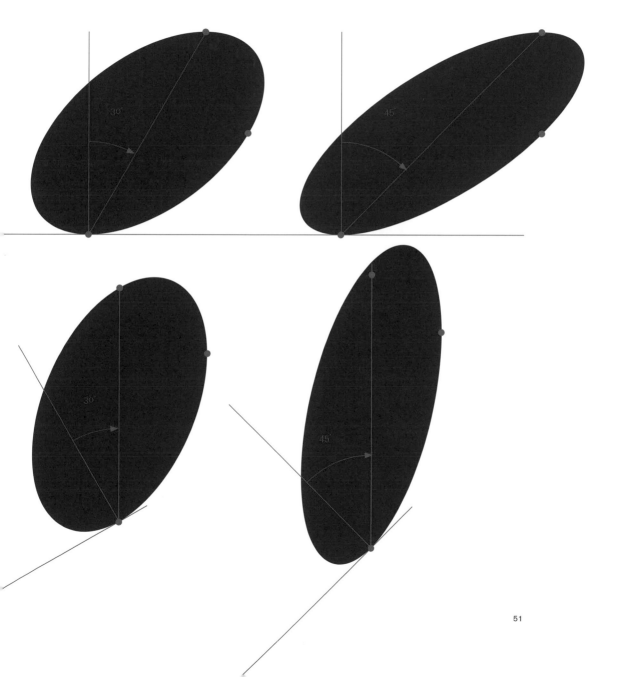

Relations

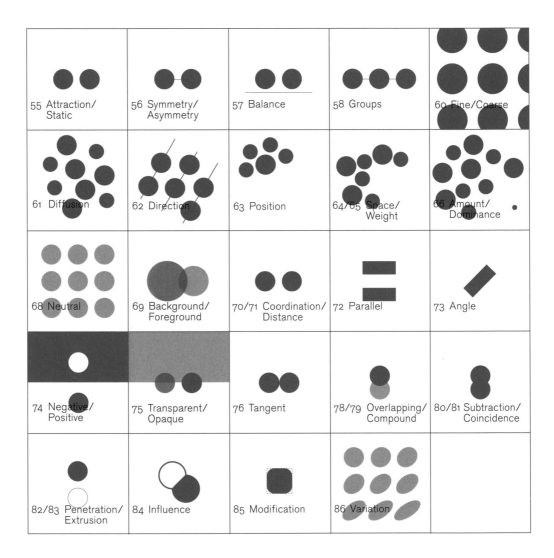

55 Attraction/
Static

56 Symmetry/
Asymmetry

57 Balance

58 Groups

60 Fine/Coarse

61 Diffusion

62 Direction

63 Position

64/65 Space/
Weight

66 Amount/
Dominance

68 Neutral

69 Background/
Foreground

70/71 Coordination/
Distance

72 Parallel

73 Angle

74 Negative/
Positive

75 Transparent/
Opaque

76 Tangent

78/79 Overlapping/
Compound

80/81 Subtraction/
Coincidence

82/83 Penetration/
Extrusion

84 Influence

85 Modification

86 Variation

Relations. Visual objects in a composition relate to the viewer, the format, and other elements within the composition.

Although this red disc sits completely motionless on a sheet of paper, forces are working on it. The object is drawn toward the margins of the page. The margins located closest to the object have the greatest impact on it. This is also the case for other elements in the composition. Elements that are closest to each other have the greatest attraction (attractive force) toward each other.

Attraction. Objects that are grouped together in a composition will either attract or repel one another.

Static. The object on page 54 is balanced and not in movement. The influential forces are equally strong and offset each other.

In a stationary representation an activity is only suggested. Energetic or lively compositions seem as if they have come to a halt or are about to initiate movement, creating an illusion of the activity before or after that moment. The composition on page 54, on the other hand, is passive or static. It is not the representation of a stopped movement. At the same time, even in a static composition there are forces at work. Note that the object must be positioned slightly above the middle of the page for the entire composition to be absolutely balanced. This is called the optical center.

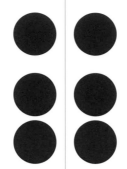

This figure is arranged
symmetrically along an axis.

Symmetry/Asymmetry. When objects are identically
arranged on both sides of an axis, they are symmetrical. An
object can be monosymmetric or multisymmetric. This page
is symmetric while the layout of the spread is asymmetric.

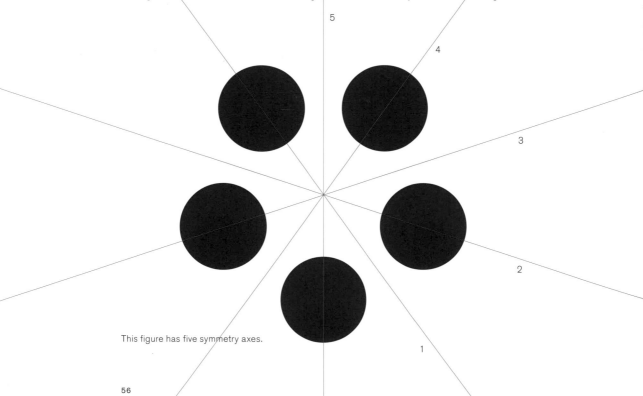

This figure has five symmetry axes.

Balance. A composition is balanced when all elements have optical equilibrium. Balance can be created between objects that have the same form but different positions, or between objects that have contrasting forms. Without this interaction between elements, a composition is static and not dynamic.

Think of this two-page layout as a composition to be balanced. The left and right pages can be compared to the arms of a scale on each side of the gutter, which acts as the tipping point. The black disc on this page offsets all the objects on the opposite page due to its larger size and the fact that it is located further out on the arm and thus has greater optical weight. In addition, there is more text on this page than on the opposite page, which further helps create balance.

Groups. When objects are repeated in a composition, they form a group, or a unit. When several units are put together, super-units are created. Groups can be named after the form of their underlying structures.

Linear group. Objects that are repeated along a line form a linear unit.

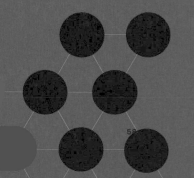

The objects in a structure composed of polygons as in the model to the left, which is formed of triangles, are made up of triangular units. The objects and the visible structure lines in this group create a texture.

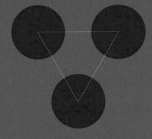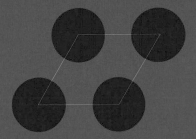

Triangular group. Objects that are repeated in
a triangular structure form a triangular unit.

Rhombic group. Objects that are
repeated in a rhombic structure form a
rhombic unit.

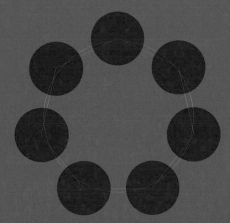

Circular group. The point at which a unit is seen as an equilateral polygon instead of a circle is a question of definition.
A polygon must have more than four sides in order to be confused with a circle. A unit can also be based on parts of a
circle; curved lines are a part of a circular form. Is the above group a seven-sided unit or a circle-based group?

This structure is coarser than...

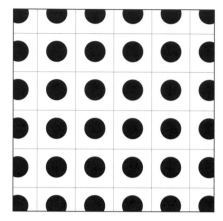

Fine/Coarse. The fineness or coarseness of a structure is determined by the distance between the structure lines. It is also relative to the distance of the viewer to the structure.

...this structure. These two structures are equally saturated but they have different degrees of fineness/coarseness.

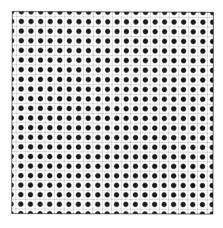

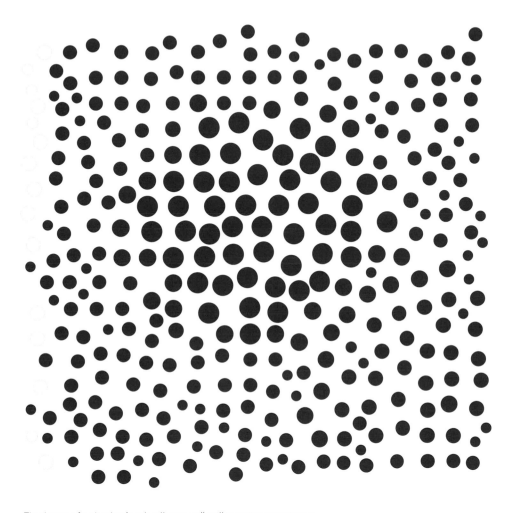

The degree of a structure's saturation as well as its coarseness can vary.

The coarseness of a dispersed field of objects is determined by the size of the objects in relation to the viewer. Its degree of saturation depends on the distance between the objects.

Diffusion. An irregular dispersion of objects in a composition is called diffusion. The structure can gradually shift from being fine to coarse, and from sparsely to highly saturated.

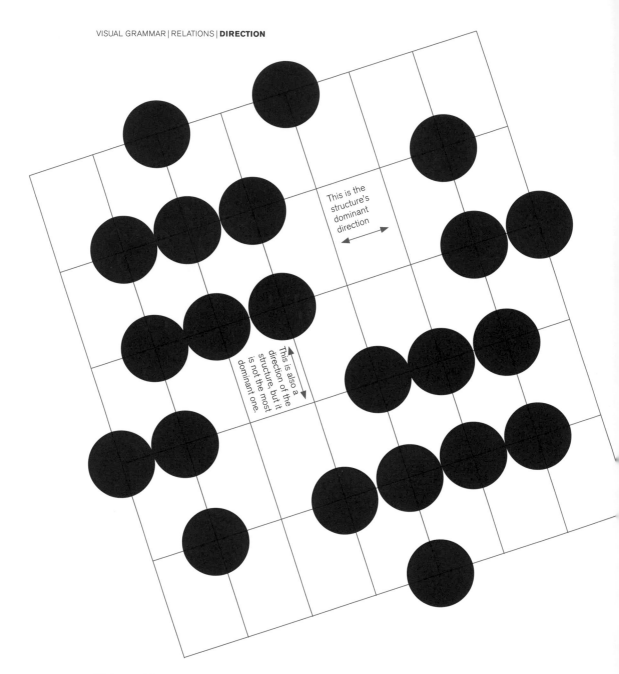

This is the structure's dominant direction

This is also a direction of the structure, but it is not the most dominant one.

Direction. A structure can actively define a direction.

Position. A group of objects can define a position in the layout, such as a corner, an edge, a center, or an optical center.

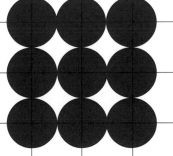

Space. A composition can have dense and open areas and in this manner create white space in the layout. The placement of objects in the structure can reinforce this impression.

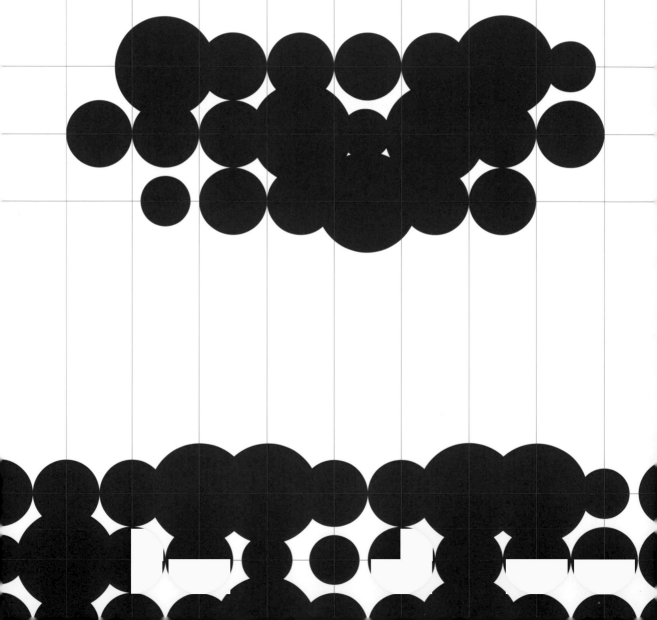

Weight. Through conscious use of the upper and lower areas of a format, the designer can play with associations of how we experience the world, alluding to the earth and the sky. The composition can create the illusion of something being light or heavy, of something that flies, or something that flows.

Amount/Dominance. A composition can have areas with many objects and areas with few objects. Areas with a large number of objects are not necessarily the most visually dominant.

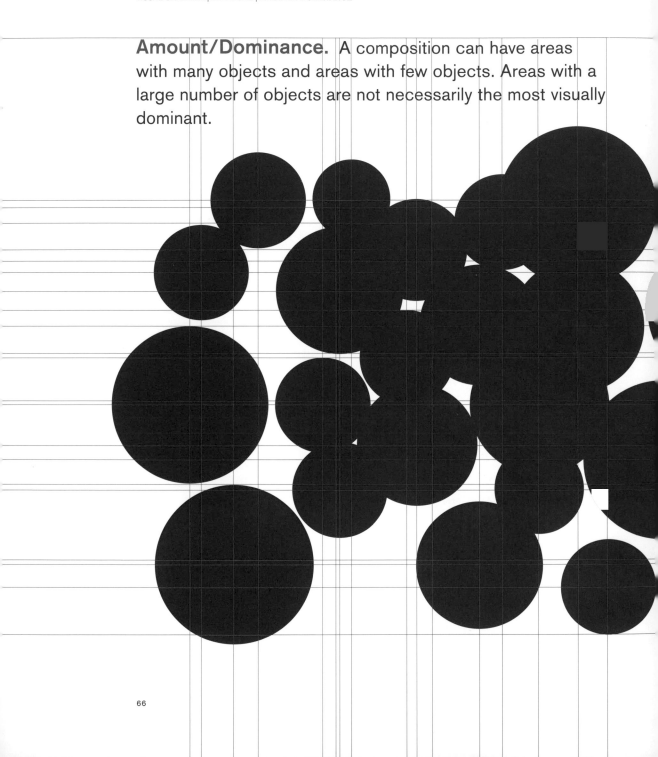

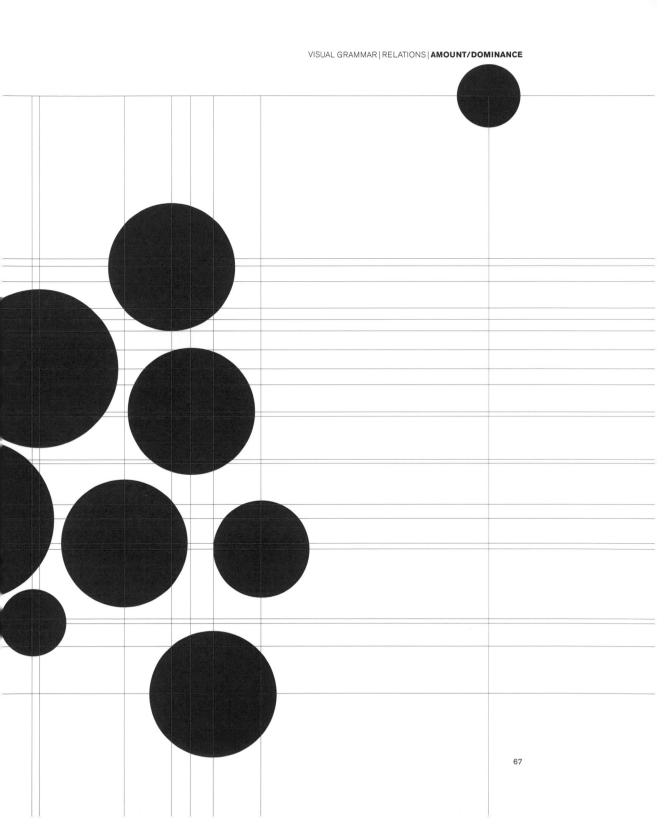

Neutral. When objects in a composition do not stand out in relation to others, they are neutral in relation to one another, and the composition as a whole can be called neutral.

The background on this page is neutral. The gray tone of the discs has a shade that is so light that it does not create a great contrast with the white background. The form does not stand out because it is a general form and because the discs are identical in size and evenly arranged.

68

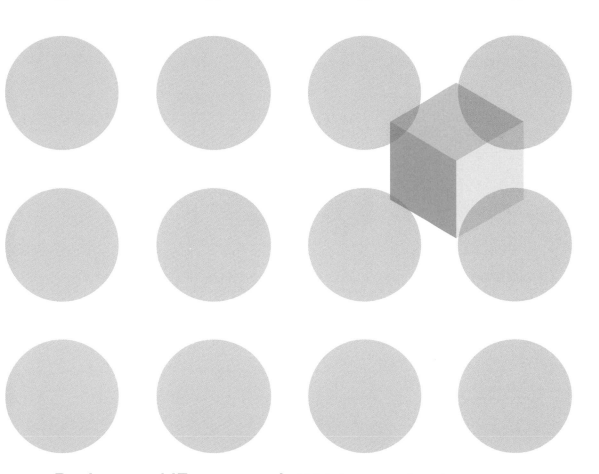

Background/ Foreground. Which parts of a picture are perceived as the background or foreground is determined by the position of the objects and their proportions in relation to one another.

Nine ways to create an impression of depth: 1. Overlapping. 2. Diagonal movement. 3. Gradually smaller/larger.
4. Abbreviation. 5. Aerial perspective (the lines of perspective converge in a vanishing point). 6. Mathematic perspective (parallel lines of perspective). 7. Colors (colors of objects far away are colder and less saturated). 8. Convergence perspective (several spaces that are parallel with the surface of the picture inwards on the depth axis). 9. Moulding (use of shade to create plastic volumes). From Gunnar Danbolt, *Blikk for bilder* (Oslo: Abstrakt forlag, 2002), 35. Summary by the author.

Coordination. Objects are coordinated, if their coordinates have the same value, the same focus, and are perceived from the same perspective.

The figures above are perceived as coordinated while the figures below are not. The bottom cube of the two illustrations below is perceived as being closer in space than the upper. When objects are seen in perspective, the element closest to the viewer is usually placed low in the composition.

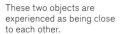

These two objects are experienced as being close to each other.

Distance. The distance perceived between two objects can vary according to the viewer's perspective. Two figures that are perceived as being close to each other can, when seen in another format, be experienced as being remote. Closeness and remoteness are relative.

The two objects on this page are experienced as being positioned far from each other. Relatively speaking, they are equally distant from each other as the two objects at the bottom of page 70.

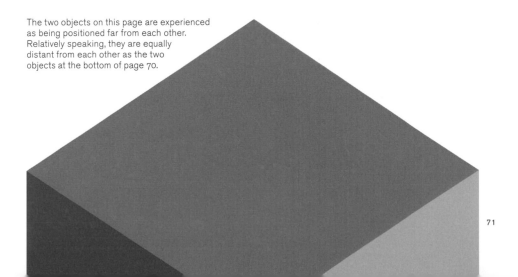

Parallel. Two lines are parallel when they lie on the same plane and are at an equal distance from each other at all times. Regardless of how long they are, they will never intersect.

Curved lines can also be parallel.

An acute angle is less than 90˚.

An obtuse angle is greater than 90˚.

A right angle is 90˚.

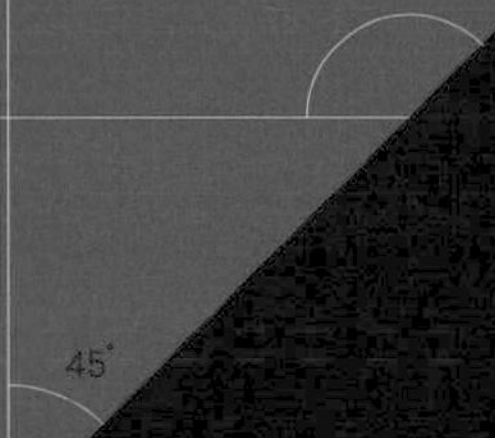

45˚

Angle. The space between two intersecting straight lines.

An object can only be situated at an angle to something else, if it has a direction. This direction is defined by the most important axis in the object's structural skeleton. (See structural skeleton on page 24.) A circle, for instance, has no direction, an ellipsis, on the other hand, does.

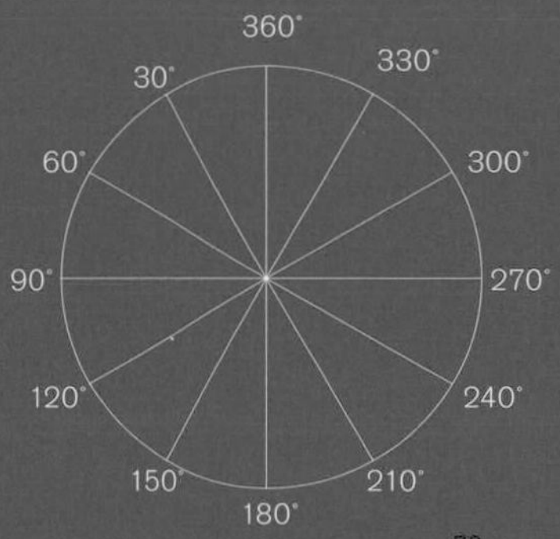

360˚
330˚
30˚
300˚
60˚
270˚
90˚
240˚
120˚
210˚
150˚
180˚

73

Negative/Positive.

The terms *negative* and *positive* relate to opposite values such as opaque and transparent, light and dark, convex and concave, solid and hollow.

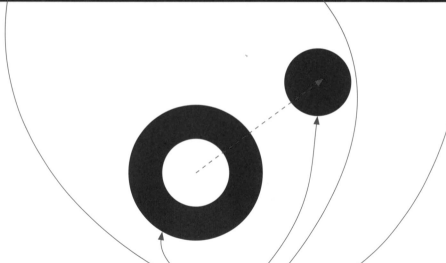

A form is called positive or negative if its tone contrasts with the surroundings. Text that is lighter than the background it is set on is negative. A positive form is extroverted (turned outward) and convex. A form that can be filled with a liquid is negative. If something is extruded from a form, the original form is positive, while the new form is negative.

Transparent/Opaque. A transparent object is see-through. Light shines through it so that other elements behind it become visible. An opaque object is visually impermeable and prevents light from shining through.

Tangent. When two objects are located next to each other and share one common point, they are called tangents.

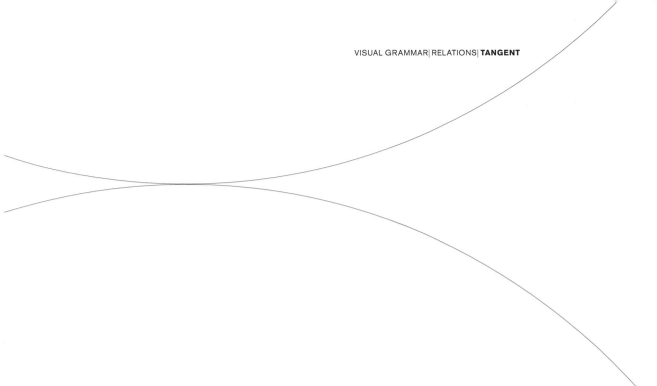

Overlapping. When parts of an object lie above parts of another object, the first object overlaps the second one.

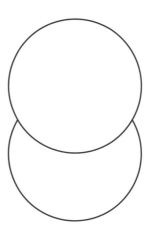

Compound. When two objects overlap each other and visually appear to be one object, the form is called a compound form.

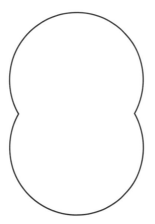

Subtraction. When the part of an object that overlaps another one is deducted from the underlying object, a subtraction has taken place.

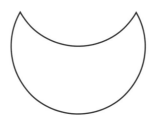

Coincidence. When two objects have the same form and size and are situated directly above one another, so that from above they appear to be one form, they coincide.

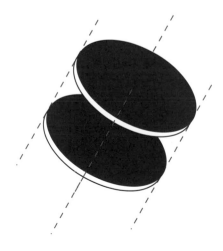

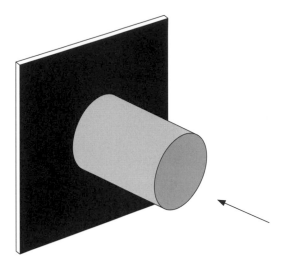

Penetration. When one object is pushed through another, larger object, a penetration has occurred.

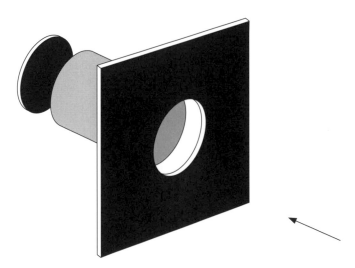

The cylinder has created a hole in the quadratic disc by penetrating it. Whether or not there was a hole in the disc previously makes little difference.

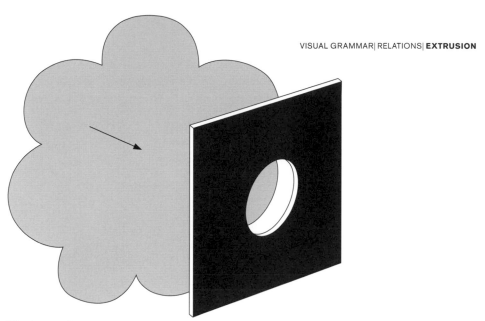

Extrusion. The process of forcing a material through an opening in an object so that the form of the opening influences the form of the material is called extruding a profile.

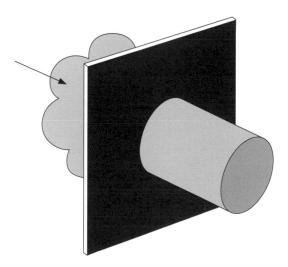

If we press a material through the hole that we penetrated on the previous page, the result will be a disc or a cylinder, depending on the amount of material pressed through. The profile acquiring the form of the opening is called the extrudate.

Influence. When an object has changed its form because of another object, it has been influenced. Objects can also mutually influence each other.

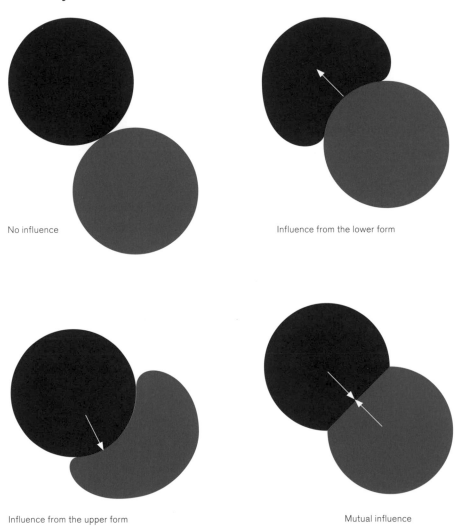

No influence

Influence from the lower form

Influence from the upper form

Mutual influence

Modification. When an object has been slightly altered, it has been modified. A modification does not change the basic characteristics of an object.

Modification can affect form, shade, hue, and texture.

Variation. Repetitions with varying and minor alterations (modifications) can be called a variation.

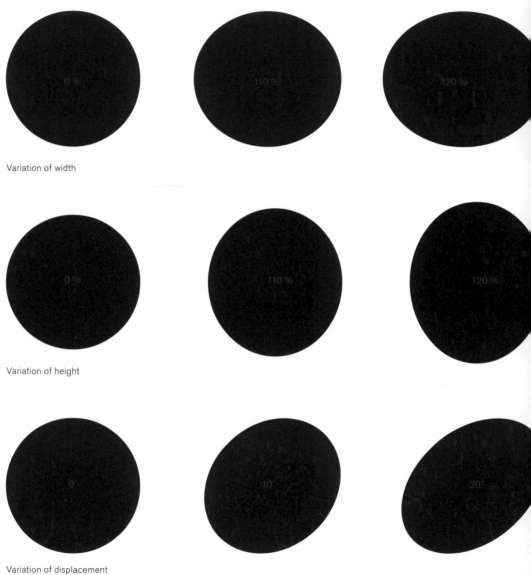

Variation of width

Variation of height

Variation of displacement

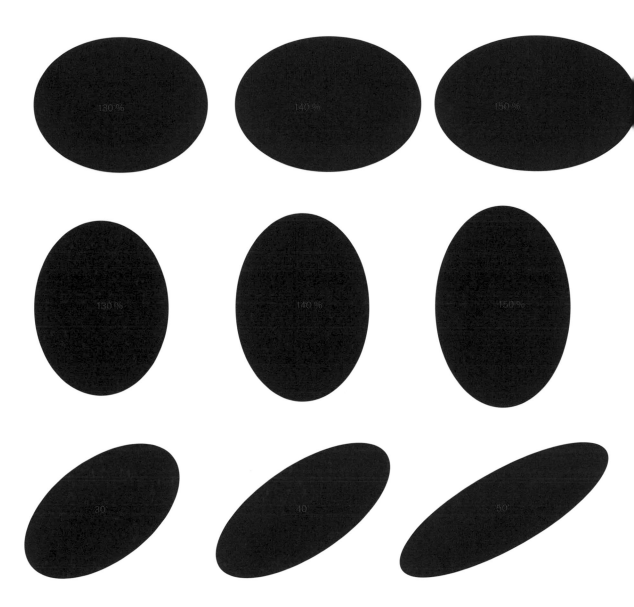

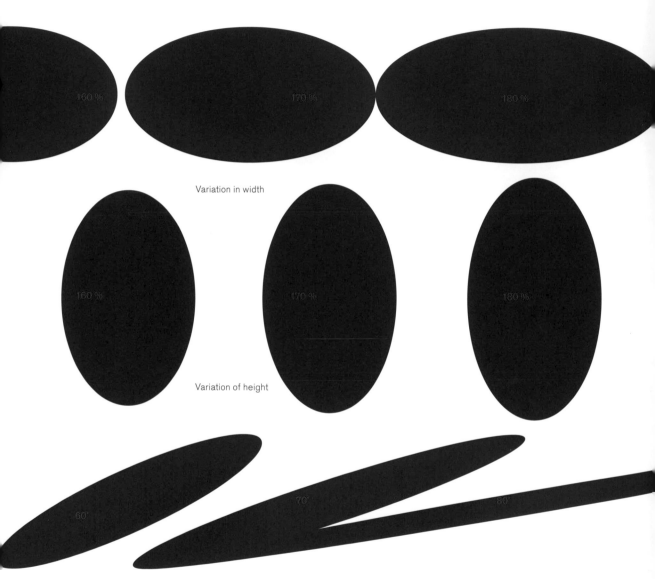

Variation in width

Variation of height

Variation of displacement

Glossary

The definitions in this glossary concern only the aesthetic and visual aspects of the terms listed here.

Abbreviation	Depiction of an object seen in perspective. Parts of the object lie outside of the composition.
Abstraction	Not real, not representing something in this world. Universal. Imagined. Underlying structures that determine the design of everything around us.
Accentuate	To stress. Emphasize. Attaching importance to one part of a whole.
Achromatic	(Of a set of colors) comprised of gray tones.
Action	Process of doing things.
Activity	In a static representation, activity is suggested. Energetic or lively poses and styles have stopped or will initiate a movement and are a representation of the activity before or after this moment.
Acute angle	An acute angle is less than 90 degrees.
Address	Indication of locality. The address can be expressed as coordinates or degrees of longitude and latitude.
Aesthetics	Teachings about the perceptible realm.
Ambiguity	Equivocal. Unclear. Obscure.
Amount	Something measurable; size, weight, number.
Analog transition	Smooth transition.
Angle	Opening between two straight intersecting lines.
Angular	(Of a state) determined by straight lines and angles; with corners.
Animated	Lively, in movement.
Application	Ornamentation applied to a base.
Apply	Affix, attach.
Arc	Part of a circle.
Asymmetric	Not symmetric. Unevenly distributed along an axis.
Attraction	Objects positioned in relative proximity to each other will always either attract or repel one another.
Axis	Imagined line. Line in a system of coordinates.
Axonometric	Reproduction in a right-angled coordinate system. A perspective without a vanishing point.
Background	Elements in a composition, whose function it is to enhance the most important objects.
Balance	Equilibrium between elements. A stability and tranquility achieved by visually positioning objects with different weights in such a way that they balance each other. Balance is a visual tension that works against and with activity.
Basic structure	Original structure.
Body	Physical entity or structure.
Bold	Fearless, with confidence, direct. With the intent of creating optimal visibility.
Bowed	Curved, bent, spherical.
Brightness	The color's position in a scale of white to black. The tone of a color.
Center	Middle point. Mathematic and optical center. Point located at the center of a format.
Centrifugal	That which tends away from a center.
Centripetal	That which tends toward a center.
Chord	Straight line between two points on a periphery.
Chromatic	(Of a set of colors) with a hued structure.
Circle	Curved line where all points have the same distance from a given point (center).
Circle terms	Arc: Part of the circumference of a circle.
	Diameter: Straight line through the center from one side of the circle to the other.
	Chord: Straight line between two points on the periphery.
	Periphery: Length around the outer edge of the circle.
	Pi: Ratio between the periphery and the diameter (approximately 3.14159).
	Radius: Distance from the center of the circle to the periphery.
	Segment: Part of the circle between a chord and the periphery.
	Sector: Part of the circle between two radii.

Circumference	Length of the contour of an object.
Close	Located a short distance away in time or space.
Coarse	Unrefined, with large texture, grained. Opposite of fine.
Coincidence	When two objects seen from a specific angle are located directly above one another.
Cold	At low temperature. Cold colors can be associated with low temperatures. Clean, sterile.
Color contrast	Hue contrast, light/dark contrast, cold/warm contrast, complementary contrast, simultaneous contrast, saturation contrast, extension contrast.
Color	Hue. Different light waves perceptible to humans, either as a result of a reflection from an object with color pigments or because the light has been filtered through a colored gas or substance and become colored light. Defined by three measurable quantities: nuance, saturation, and tone.
Combination	Connection, amalgamation, arrangement of several items in a set order.
Communication	Exchange of messages between a sender and a receiver.
Complementary	Supplementary. In reference to pairs of colors that give an impression of white when perceived by the eye simultaneously.
Complex	Composed of several elements and forces. Visually intricate. A pattern that is difficult to discern or understand.
Composition	Mixture, combination, organizing different visual elements into a whole.
Compound	When two objects have a common circumference.
Concave	Curved or bowed inward, bowl-shaped. Opposite of convex. A concave angle is less than 180°.
Concentric	With a common center.
Consistent	A composition dominated by identical or similar elements.
Constant	Unchanging, lasting, unbroken, continuous.
Contour	Outline. The line that encloses the form.
Contrast	The opposite of harmony. For something to be full of contrast, it must have characteristics that stand out in relation to something else. The contrasting elements are mutually dependent. Types of contrasts can be broken down into three main types: tone, color, and form.
Convergent perspective	Impression of depth created by several spaces positioned parallel with the surface, and inward on the depth axis.
Convex	Curved or bowed outward. Arched. The opposite of concave. A convex angle is greater than 180°.
Coordinate	Numerical quantity, length of one, two, or three lines determining the location of a point.
Coordinated	Expresses the interaction between two elements or more and the comparable relation between them.
Cube	Physical entity delimited by six equally large squares. Dice, cubus.
Curve	Bowed line, arch, bend.
Dark	Absence of light.
Deformation	Change of form. Change of the normal form. Malformation.
Delineated	Distinct. Of form that has great contrast and a clear division between contrasting elements.
Density	Mass over volume. Also applies to format composition and tone extensions in a picture or raster.
Depth	Depth is a visual illusion that can be achieved with the help of perspective. Depth can also by expressed by color depth or tone depth. Transparent elements that partially conceal others can also create the illusion of depth.
Depth axis	Dimension in a composition that refers to the axis leading inward on a format.
Design	Action, industry, and product. Development of an object/process so it functions according to the intentions.
Diagonal	Straight line from one corner to the opposite corner of a rectangle.
Diameter	Straight line through the center from one side of a circle to the other.
Diffusion	Irregular dispersion of small elements or light.
Dimension	Extension in space and time. Size, scope.
Direction	Objects in a composition will always, except when they are centered, indicate a movement in a direction. Objects can also, based on their placement in relation to other objects, be placed on a line that has a direction. An object can also indicate a direction on the basis of its own form (structural skeleton) .
Disc	Thin, flat, and round surface. Plate that appears to be two-dimensional.
Displaced	An object (or parts of it) that is moved away from its proper position.
Dissemination	Spreading, distribution.
Distance	Space between two points or places.
Distinct	Striking, noteworthy, prominent.

Distort	Push, twist, or turn inside out.
Distribution	Apportionment, diffusion.
Dominant	Particularly prominent. Makes its presence felt over that of others.
Dynamic	Teachings about the movement of bodies under the influence of energy. Creates and reduces tension between objects in a visual composition.
Economical	Frugal in use of elements to emphasize purity and simplicity.
Edge	Transition from one area to another. The enclosure of an object.
Element	One of the units comprising a quantity. Components contributing to the creation of a whole.
Endpoint	The end of a line (chord).
Enlargement	A reproduction that is larger than the original.
Episodic	(Of repetition with frequency) a repetition that varies; repetition with breaks.
Even	By removing or decreasing the effects that can create depth (perspective, light/shade, transparency), one will arrive at something that appears even.
Extrovert	Outwardly oriented.
Extrudate	The form brought about by forcing a material through an opening.
Eye level	Light waves that meet the eye at a right angle.
Fine	Refined, pure, thin, small-grained. Opposite of coarse.
Force	Strength, power, energy.
Form	A contour of an object in a plane defines its form. All forms are defined by contours created by infinite combinations of straight and curved lines.
Formal	Having to do with the form. Pertaining to outer form. In accordance with the forms. Without content.
Format	The concrete surroundings in or upon which the visual elements shall function. This can be the size of a sheet of paper or the type of medium by which signals are transported.
Fractal	Irregular form that lies outside of the realm of classical geometry.
Fragmentary	Broken up, divided into a number of parts. In pieces, disjointed, split up.
Frame	The line surrounding a format.
Freeform	A form that is difficult to categorize; organic.
Frequency	Rate. Frequent occurrence.
Fusion	When two or more units join to make one.
Geometry	Mathematic teachings about points, lines, surfaces, and solids and their mutual relations in space.
Gestalt (n)	Figure, shape.
Gestalt (v)	To form, produce, give life to.
Glossy	(Of the character of a surface) a surface that is so smooth and shiny that objects are reflected in it.
Golden section	Proportion between two lengths where the ratio of the shortest to the longest is the same as that of the longest to the whole. This ratio is 1.618.
Gradation	Gradual change. Used in reference to a tone or texture's increasing or decreasing saturation, or to an object's increasing or decreasing size, either through repetition or by way of perspective.
Grammar	Teachings about the structure of language, the elements comprising it, and the rules of their combination.
Gravity	Force drawing objects towards the center of the Earth.
Grid	Module system, skeleton, structure. Dividing the composition into smaller compositions that determine the design of the object or the placement of elements in the format.
Group	Unit made up of elements positioned together or with a shared characteristic so they are associated with one another.
Half-tone	Hue in the gray tone scale, between black and white.
Handmade	Directly influenced by human hands.
Harmony	When several elements are put together creating a state of balance. Contrast is a force in opposition to harmony, but contrast and harmony will always function together. A harmony can be full of contrasts and contrasts can be harmonious.
Hexagram	Rectilinear figure delimited by six sides.
Highlight	The lightest part of a half-tone or color picture.
Horizon	Line where the sky and Earth or surface of the ocean meet. Limit of knowledge or vision, vista.
Horizontal	Level. Opposite of vertical (perpendicular).
Hypercube	Volume with more than three dimensions.

Identical	Alike, one and the same, equivalent to.
Inactive	Idle, without activity.
Incunabulum	Book printed between 1450 and 1500.
Influence	To change one thing through the force or power of something else.
Informal	Not applying to form. That which does not preserve form. Opposite of formal.
Inscription	Engraving.
Intersection	Where two axes have a common point. Origo.
Introverted	Inwardly oriented. Opposite of extroverted.
Invisible	That which cannot be seen by the eye.
Irregular	(Of design) with emphasis on the unexpected or unusual, without following a clear or comprehensible plan.
Isolated	(Of a composition about a single element) not supported by other visual stimuli.
Kinetics	Teachings of movement, dynamics.
Labile	Unstable, inconstant, insecure. Lack of balance, unpleasant and disturbing composition.
Light	Electromagnetic rays that cause sense impressions in the human eye. Opposite of dark.
Line	A line in its abstract form consists of points situated next to one another in one direction. If the line has a defined start and endpoint, it is called a vector. A line is the shortest distance between two points. In its concrete form a line is a surface with extreme contrast between length and width. Lines or strokes are often used to enhance the difference in tone or hue between two surfaces.
Linear	Shaped as a line.
Majority	Plurality. The opposite of minority.
Matrix	Deep casting mould, negative print. Arrangement of elements in rows and columns (horizontally and vertically).
Matt	A surface character that causes light to spread on the surface. Opposite of glossy.
Minority	Smaller amount. Opposite of majority.
Mirror image	Where left and right, and up and down are reversed. An object inverted through a line or surface.
Model	Prototype, pattern.
Modification	Minor adjustment.
Module	Basic element.
Movement	In visual communication movement is either represented or an illusion of movement is created. In a two-dimensional still image, representations of movement are achieved through composition and technique. An illusion of movement is created by showing objects with slightly different placements at high frequency, so the eye is deceived into believing that the object moves.
Multi-dimensional	Having several dimensions. One can define objects with more than three dimensions but as humans we cannot see or feel them.
Negative form	A hollow shape. When something is brighter than something else.
Neutral	Not belonging to any extreme. Located between extremes. When no elements are prominent.
Object	Element forming the basis for a conception or idea.
Obtuse angle	An obtuse angle is greater than 90°.
One-dimensional	Having one dimension. This is an abstract state because all physical objects have three dimensions.
Opaque	Obscure, impermeable. Opposite of transparent.
Optic	Teachings about light and visual phenomena.
Origo	Point of departure, intersection between axes.
Oval	Oblong circle.
Overlap	When parts of an object lie above parts of another object, then one object overlaps the other.
Parallel	Running in the same direction, concurrent, side by side. Of two lines or planes that never meet, no matter how far their extension.
Path	Imagined line along which an object is moving. The path can be straight or curved.
Pattern	Ornaments, characteristic features of something.
Peak	Zenith of an angle between two or more lines or surfaces.
Pendulum	A body that can swing on a fixed axis.
Penetrate	Force through, enter, or seep into.
Pentagon	Regular five-sided figure.

Periphery	Circumference, outer edge, outskirts, length around the edge of a circle.
Perpendicular	An angle of 90°.
Perspective	Manner of depiction that creates the impression of depth.
Place (v)	To affix in a specific place.
Plastic	Product with three-dimensional form.
Point	An abstract phenomenon indicating a precise location. Place without area. Smallest typographical unit of measure. 1/12 Cicero. Abbreviated as pt. One point is 0.0148 inches.
Point of departure	Origo.
Polygon	Multiangular, multilateral.
Position	Pose, standpoint, location.
Precision	Concrete representation of our visual surroundings; illustrates that all objects have an innate wealth of detail.
Primary colors	Basic colors. Colors that cannot be created by mixing other colors.
Projection	Depiction of one or more points on a line. Representation of a body on a plane.
Proportion	Relation of one thing to another. Correlation in scale.
Radiation	Light emission, emanation. Distribution from a center.
Radius	Distance from the center of a circle to the periphery.
Random	(Of irregular variations) not following any cycle or fixed pattern.
Raster	A structure with points distributed on a surface.
Rearrange	To relocate something.
Rectangle	Four-sided figure with four right angles.
Reflection	Return of a wave-movement from a surface. Mirroring.
Regularity	Design using uniform elements; design using a fixed plan or pattern.
Relation	Ratio, connection.
Relative	Seen in relation to something else, compared with something else.
Remote	Located far away in time or space.
Rendering	To cover the surface of a three-dimensional object.
Repetition	When an element recurs several times, either in a composition or over time.
Representation	One thing standing for another.
Repulsion	Force increasing the distance between objects. Opposite of attraction.
Rhomb	Parallelogram with sides of equal length, but whose angles need not be right angles.
Rhythm	Movement measured in time. Repetition in groups.
Rotation	An object's revolution around an axis.
Rubric	A category or column in a table.
Saturation	The intensity of a color's hue. In unsaturated colors, some of the color has been replaced by white or black.
Scaled down	A reproduction that is smaller than the original.
Secondary color	A color derived by mixing two primary colors.
Sector	The part of a circle that lies between two radii.
Segment	The part of a circle that is defined by a chord and the periphery.
Semiology	Study of signs.
Shade	Specific color tone or gray tones. Can also describe a texture.
Shadow	Where light does not fall upon an object.
Simple	Direct and elementary, the interplay between forms characterized by order. Visual elements without distortions or amplifications can be called simple.
Simultaneous	At the same time.
Size	The relative area or length of an object measured against another object or a scale of measurement.
Skeleton	Organization, plan, theory. Framework upon which one can build.
Space	Three-dimensional geometric term, volume delimited by a surface or surfaces.
Sphere	Physical entity where all points on the surface are at an equal distance from the center. Globe. Scope, realm, surroundings.
Spiral	Curve revolving around a point several times as it distances itself from that point.

Spontaneous	With obvious lack of plan or pattern, emotional, impulsive, and without inhibition.
Starting point	Point of departure, beginning.
Static	Stationary and in absolute equilibrium.
Stratum	Layer, plane.
Stroke	Physical, concrete line. Extremely narrow surface.
Structural skeleton	An object's inner structure. Structure lines in a form.
Structure	Composition, inner nature; the way a whole is put together out of different parts.
Structure line	The one or numerous (visible or invisible) lines that distinguish the individual structure units from one another.
Structure unit	Area in a structure that can hold an element.
Subtle	Refined and sophisticated.
Subtract	To take away.
Super-unit	An entity that is composed of several units.
Surface	The outside of a volume or an object.
Symbol	Object, sign, or image representing something.
Symmetrical	That which can be divided into two equal parts comprising mirror images of each other. Arrangement along an axis.
Tactile	Relating to the sense of touch.
Tangent	Touch, border on, brush against, of two objects with a common point (point of tangency).
Texture	Texture can be the concrete expression of a structure. A texture is a distribution of objects in a composition that is so even that it is experienced as part of a surface. Texture can be experienced both tactilely and visually.
Three-dimensional	Having three dimensions. All physical objects have three dimensions.
Tone	Characteristic of an object based on how much light falls on it and how it is reflected. Tone is our most important impression of an object's form, size, and position in terms of orientation.
Torso	Body, trunk.
Transparent	Lucid, permeable. Opposite of opaque.
Triangle	Three-sided figure.
Triangular	Three-sided.
Two-dimensional	Having two dimensions. This is an abstract state because all physical objects have three dimensions.
Understatement	Cautious statement. Attempt to create maximum response from a viewer through minimum use of effects.
Uniform	When several objects fit together in such a way as to create balance and be perceived as a totality.
Unit	Object or group of objects presumed to be complete in and of themselves.
Value	An object's value stems from a subjective assessment of its characteristics.
Variable	Quantity with changeable value.
Variation	Composition that changes around a dominant theme.
Vertex	Summit or meeting point.
Vertical	Perpendicular. Opposite of horizontal (level).
Visible	Perceivable by the eye.
Visual	In reference to sight.
Visual syntax	The composition of objects.
Void	Vacuum.
Volume	The space within a three-dimensional body.
Warm	With a high temperature. Warm colors can be associated with high temperatures. Vigorous, natural. Opposite of cold.
Weight	Force that influences the mass of an object and its gravity towards the Earth's center.
Zenith	Vertex.

Bibliography

Abbott, Edwin A.   *Flatland.* New York: New American Library, 1984. First published by London: Seeley & Co, 1884.

Arnheim, Rudolf.   *Art and Visual Perception.* Berkeley: University of California Press, 1954.

Banchoff, Thomas F.   *Beyond the Third Dimension.* New York: Scientific American Library, 1990.

Berger, John.   *Ways of Seeing.* London: Penguin Books, 1972.

Broby-Johansen, R.   *Kunstordbog.* Viborg: Forlaget Sesam, 2000.

Danbolt, Gunnar.   *Blikk for bilder.* Oslo: Abstrakt forlag, 2002.

Davidsen, Stein.   *Grafisk håndbok.* Oslo: Yrkesopplæring, 1995.

Dondis A. Dondis.   *A Primer of Visual Literacy.* Cambridge: MIT Press, 1973.

Fletcher, Alan.   *The Art of Looking Sideways.* London: Phaidon Press, 2001.

Garrett, Lillian.   *Visual Design.* New York: Reinhold, 1967.

Guttu, Tor, ed.   *Norsk ordbok.* Oslo: Kunnskapsforlaget, 1998.

Itten, Johannes.   *The Art of Color.* New York: Reinhold, 1967.

Hellmark, Christer.   *Bokstaven, ordet, texten.* Stockholm: Ordfront forlag, 1997.

Horn, Robert.   *Visual Language.* Bainbridge Island: MacRovu Inc, 1999.

Hornby, A. S., ed.   *Advanced Learner's Dictionary of Current English.* Oxford: Oxford University Press, 1974.

Kandinsky, Wassily.   *Point and Line to Plane.* New York: Dover, 1979. First published at Bauhaus, 1926

Koestler, Arthur.   *The Act of Creation.* London: Hutchinson & Co, 1964.

Krausse, J., ed.   *Your Private Sky, R. Buckminster Fuller.* Baden: Lars Müller Publishers, 1999.

Kress, Gunther, ed.   *Reading Images. The Grammar of Visual Design.* London: Routledge, 1996.

Kruger, Anna, ed.   *Faktikon.* Oslo: Gyldendal, 1997.

Liungman, Carl C.   *Symboler.* Malmö: Aldebaran Förlag, 1990.

Tveterås, Egil, ed.   *Ettbindsleksikon.* Oslo: Kunnskapsforlaget, 1985.

Winters, Nathan.   *Architecture is Elementary.* Layton: Gibbs M. Smith, 1986.

Wong, Wucius.   *Principles of Form and Design.* New York: Van Nostrand Reinhold, 1993.

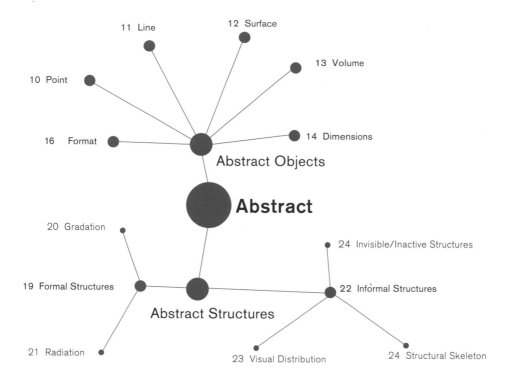

11 Line
12 Surface
13 Volume
10 Point
16 Format
14 Dimensions

Abstract Objects

Abstract

20 Gradation
24 Invisible/Inactive Structures
19 Formal Structures
22 Informal Structures

Abstract Structures

21 Radiation
23 Visual Distribution
24 Structural Skeleton

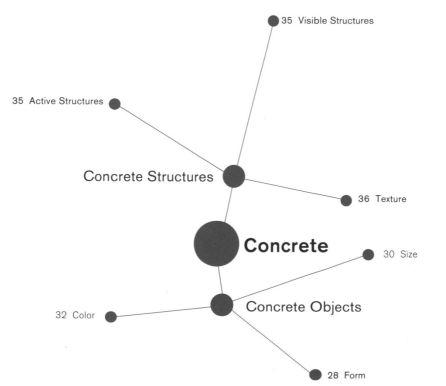

35 Visible Structures
35 Active Structures

Concrete Structures

36 Texture

Concrete
30 Size

32 Color

Concrete Objects

28 Form